The B.G.C Formula: Belief.Grind.Consistency

Written By: Ebony The Ebonizer

Dedication

This book is dedicated to every person who strives for something greater and to reach newer heights. Your belief, grind, and consistency will take you to places you never imagined.

Foreword

If you're reading this, consider yourself blessed and ready to gain the knowledge needed to elevate your life. When I first heard about this novel, I wondered—how could my wife possibly surpass her previous masterpiece, *Self Identity*? If you haven't read that one yet, I highly recommend doing so first, then coming back to this one to fully immerse yourself in the **Ebonized** movement.

To my wife, Ebony—I am beyond proud of you. You continue to use your passion, purpose, and gifts to create a space where people can truly grow and transform. The fact that you've taken this novel a step deeper into enlightenment and self-discovery is nothing short of incredible. Having read it, I wholeheartedly believe this book will help many people unlock the next level of their journey and experience life to the fullest.

To the readers—buckle up and get ready to be **Ebonized!** Ebony is about to take you on a powerful journey toward greatness. I remember when we shared this affirmation:

"I will do great things. I am great. And I will make those around me great."

These words hold universal power, and I challenge you to speak them daily—over yourself, your loved ones, and your future. This novel will equip you with everything you need to embody this mindset. It's insightful, inspiring, humorous at times, and deeply transformative.

Before you begin, I encourage you to pray. Ask for wisdom and an open heart to receive the life-changing insights within these pages.

Ebony, I love you beyond words. Now, go give the people everything you've got—it's time for belief, grind, and consistency.

Amen,

Jeff Baylock
Proud Husband

Introduction

As a child, even at the tender age of four, I felt a deep-seated desire to become an entertainer. It all started when I first heard the angelic voice of Whitney Houston and the rich, soothing vocals of Toni Braxton. Their ability to captivate audiences with their voices fascinated me to no end. From that moment, I resolved to use my voice to evoke similar emotions in people. Whether it was a gift from God or mere coincidence that my parents named me after the famous singer Shanice, I found solace and purpose in my ability to sing.

However, as I grew older, I faced numerous obstacles, hardships, and bouts of self-doubt. I lacked self-confidence and often felt overwhelmed by financial instability and lack of support. At times, it seemed like there was no end in sight to my struggles.

Have you ever found yourself alone, contemplating your life, and suddenly feeling a wave of uncertainty over you? I experienced one of those **"What the hell am I doing?"** moments. I had become complacent, comfortable with living in doubt and uncertainty, and had lost sight of the dreams and goals I had as a child.

Many of us are in a similar position, afraid to step out of our comfort zones and take risks. But life, I realized, is about embracing uncertainty and having faith. To achieve greatness, we must be willing to make sacrifices and take bold steps forward.

This is not just another motivational speech or book. I'm not here to motivate you; I'm here to awaken you. Many of you have been asleep too long, ignoring your gifts and losing sight of your purpose.

When I realized I was letting my purpose slip away, I knew I had to take action. But I didn't know where to start or what to do. I wanted to be a boss, an entertainer, a speaker, but I lacked a roadmap for how to get there.

So, I began studying successful people in my inner circle and the world of celebrities. I noticed a typical pattern among them—a formula for success called **The B.G.C. Formula: Belief, Grind, Consistency**. When I applied this formula to my own life, my circumstances began to change dramatically, and this is why today, I'm happily married, pursuing a thriving career in music and speaking, and running multiple businesses.

But let me be clear: implementing this formula is not easy. It requires hard work, dedication, and perseverance. In this book, I'll break down the B.G.C. Formula and show you what it takes to truly believe in yourself, grind through the challenges, and stay consistent in pursuing your goals.

If you've made it this far, I hope you're ready to learn and take action to change your circumstances. I hope you're ready to unleash the potential within you and reclaim control of your life. So enough with the motivational talk—let's roll up our sleeves and start learning this formula.

Part I: BELIEF

When you hear the word **"believe,"** what's the first thing that comes to mind? Is it a catchy song that pumps you up? Maybe it's a podcast that gets you motivated, or a powerful speech by your favorite speaker that lights a fire within you. But let me share my perspective with you—I believe that **"believe"** is one of the most misunderstood, misused, and overused words out there. Why? It's simple. Many toss it around without truly understanding its context. And even more importantly, most people don't know how to truly embody belief.

Think about it. Throughout your life, you've probably been told countless times that you need to believe in yourself. Maybe you've attended empowering conferences or listened to motivational speakers who got you all fired up, ready to conquer the world. You leave feeling energized, with a newfound sense of purpose. But then, after a few days, that feeling fades. You find yourself slipping back into old habits and routines.

Now, you might be wondering, **"Are these empowerment events and speakers ineffective?"** Not at all. They serve a purpose—they ignite a spark within you, urging you to take action. But here's the thing: once that spark is lit, you need something to keep it burning. Otherwise, it'll fizzle out.

Think of it like this: It's like handing someone the keys to a car and expecting them to drive without teaching them how, or telling someone they can swim but neglecting to teach them the basics. Without proper guidance and support, failure is inevitable.

The point I'm trying to make is this: how can we expect to believe in ourselves if we've never been taught how? Many of you reading this may be facing tough times or uncertain circumstances. The idea of belief might seem unrealistic given your current situation. Without the right tools and mindset, belief can feel like nothing more than a distant dream.

Trust me, I've been there. I've questioned how I could believe in myself when I didn't know how to pay my bills or escape a hostile environment. However, dwelling on excuses and limitations only held me back. Instead, I shifted my mindset to focus on why I could succeed.

I reached a point where I was tired of making excuses and playing the blame game. I knew I had untapped potential that I couldn't afford to waste, so I decided to take action. And that's where the **B.G.C. formula** came into play. By breaking down each word—**Belief, Grind, Consistency**—I developed a system to apply to my life daily.

So, let's dive deeper into the word **"belief."** Together, we'll uncover what it truly means and how we can embody it. Because when we believe in ourselves, anything is possible.

Belief. What does the word indeed mean? When I ask this question to others, they often respond with lofty, philosophical answers, attempting to delve into deep interpretations. But can I be honest? It's not really that deep; it's relatively simple. Belief is an **action, a verb,** something you set into motion. Belief is the process of converting positive energy into action through logical reasoning.

What do I mean by logical reasoning? Let me illustrate with an example. Imagine someone claiming to believe they are a chicken. A chicken? That sounds absurd, doesn't it? Of course, it does. Because even though this person "believes" they are a chicken, is it logical? Of course not. That's precisely the point. Everyone has the right to believe in whatever they want, but without logical reasoning, that positive energy disappears. In other words, belief is positive energy that needs to be channeled into a concept that you logically put into action to fulfill your purpose.

So you may be wondering, **"Ebony, what happens when we don't use the belief system properly?"** I'm glad you asked—let me break it down for you with a real-world example.

Meet **John**, a 35-year-old entrepreneur who is **all in on the idea of manifestation**. He truly believes that if he just **thinks rich, riches will come**. Every day, he follows social media gurus preaching that **mindset alone** is the key to success, convincing himself that hard work and strategy are secondary.

But here's the problem—**John isn't actually doing the work**. Instead of developing a **real business strategy**, making **smart financial decisions**, and actually **executing his ideas**, he spends his days journaling affirmations, meditating on millions, and **waiting** for success to magically appear. He avoids the **uncomfortable but necessary tasks** like **marketing, networking, and refining his sales process**. Even worse, he ignores his **financial responsibilities**, assuming that **"the universe will provide."**

The fallout? **His business flops** because hope isn't a strategy. He **racks up debt**, believing positive vibes alone will pay the bills. Instead of taking ownership of his mistakes, he blames **"low vibrations" and "bad energy"** for his failure. And when his business doesn't work out, he

pivots to selling manifestation coaching—despite never having achieved financial success himself. Now, he's leading **others** down the same dead-end road.

This isn't just a **John** problem—it's a **big business problem**. The **self-help industry is worth over $13 billion**, but many so-called **"coaches" misuse belief systems** to sell false hope. They promise **overnight success, abundance without work, or spiritual shortcuts to wealth**, leading people to invest in programs that don't deliver. The reality? **92% of individuals fail to achieve their goals**, according to research from the **University of Scranton**. This high failure rate proves that **setting goals without a real plan and execution isn't enough**.

This is what happens when **belief without action takes over**. Having a strong mindset is great, but without **execution, strategy, and accountability**, it's just **wishful thinking**. Success isn't about waiting—it's about

working, adjusting, and staying committed to the process.

If you want to create **real success**, you need to **establish an adequate belief system that actually works**—one that balances **mindset, action, and strategy**.

So, with that in mind, **there are FOUR steps to establishing an adequate belief system:**

Step I: Establish a P.W.R: What is a PWR? Simple.

Purpose – The True Intent

The **big picture** behind everything. Purpose is the **core mission**, the reason something exists beyond just making money or gaining success. It's about **impact, legacy, and transformation**.

Key Question: What's the ultimate goal or higher meaning?

Why – The Driving Force

This is the **fire in your soul**—the deep, personal, and emotional **fuel** behind your actions. Your "why" keeps you

committed when things get tough and turns a vision into a **movement**.

Key Question: What deep emotional, spiritual, or personal force drives you?

Reason – The Solid Foundation

The **facts, logic, and experience** that validate your purpose. It's the **proof, wisdom, and evidence** that backs up why this belief or path makes sense. It keeps you **grounded and unshakable**.

Key Question: What experiences, data, or logic justify this?

How It All Connects:

PURPOSE: gives direction.

WHY: fuels the mission.

REASON: keeps it solid.

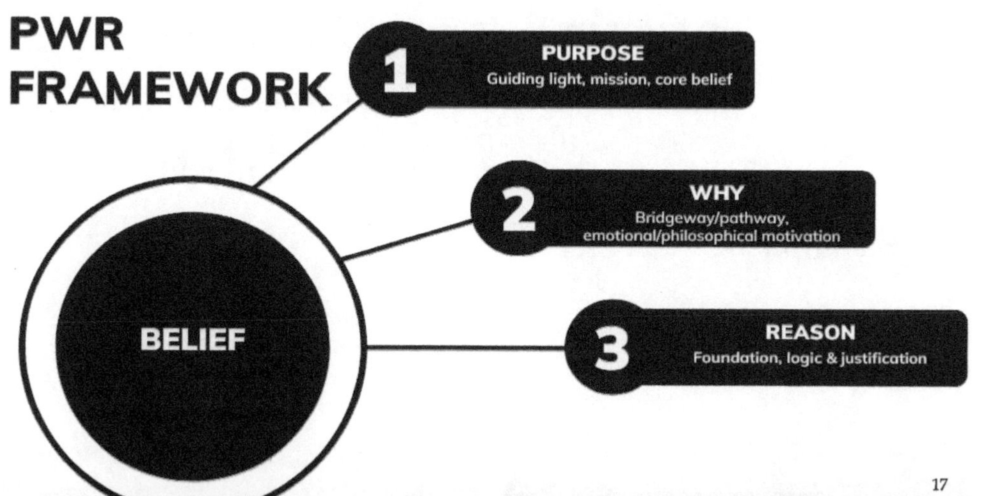

Each time you decide to believe in something, whether it's an aspiration, person, idea, etc., you must establish a PWR to provide logical reasoning. You can have many beliefs, but support them all with a PWR. For example, as a child, I wanted to be a famous entertainer. However, you cannot become famous overnight, so I needed to back my belief with logical reasoning. Here's how my PWR would look: **Purpose:** I want to establish a record label to generate a sustainable income. **Why:** This purpose will allow me to promote, market, and advertise my music and brand effectively, establishing myself as a worldwide entertainer. **Reason:** With this motivation, I can accomplish this due to my experience in entertainment, educational background, certifications, and business knowledge.

As you delve into my PWR, notice how I shift my desire to **"be famous"** into a more logical reason. This makes my goal more accessible because it lessens the pressure I put on myself and clarifies what I truly aim to accomplish.

This is why establishing a PWR is essential. It offers insight into what we seek and provides the clarity we need. Often, after pursuing beliefs, I realized I was truly after something else, not what I initially thought. So, take the time to create your own PWR. If you can't do it alone, seek guidance from trusted family members, friends, mentors, etc. You cannot skip over this step if you want to establish a genuine belief system.

Step II: Eliminate Negative Mechanisms:

Unfortunately, we all develop bad habits over the years that become ingrained in our daily routines. The problem is that we fall into such a pattern that we don't realize the adverse effects these habits have on our lives.

For example, many of us suffer from being double-minded. I must admit, at one point, I was double-minded as well. What does double-minded mean? It means being indecisive, wavering, and inconsistent. Simply put, you cannot focus.

Double-mindedness hinders the goals you set for yourself and creates negative mechanisms in your life. This is just one example of a bad habit/mechanism. For some, it may be procrastination; for others, it could be as simple as not getting enough rest or consuming the wrong foods that drain your energy. The point is, whatever your bad habit is, you must replace it with a positive one to eliminate negative mechanisms.

Let's take gossiping as an example of a bad habit. To gossip, you have to be around people who enjoy gossiping. Here's the thing about gossiping: First, you make judgments or assumptions based on rumors, not facts, which gives you an unfair outlook on people or situations. Second, gossiping creates negative energy that ultimately breeds a negative environment. This negative energy converts into procrastination, serving as a distraction that can lead you away from your reality and goals.

So, how do you stop gossiping? It's simple. **STOP** entertaining it. Surround yourself with positive people who share similar goals and aspirations as you, and turn that bad habit into a positive one.

Another aspect to consider is that some bad habits are learned behaviors passed down from generation to generation until someone decides to break the cycle. For example, lack of financial literacy is a common "bad habit" passed down through families because previous generations weren't taught about financial literacy. This lack of knowledge puts individuals at risk of not achieving their goals.

So, how do we break bad habits? It's simple. Decide to eliminate those bad habits by educating yourself on ways to break them and replacing them with positive habits. We decide to step out of our old ways and be willing to learn something new to achieve different results and establish positive mechanisms.

Step III: Establish Daily Positive Reinforcements:

Once you eliminate negative mechanisms, the next step is establishing daily positive reinforcements. What is positive reinforcement? It's rewarding positive behavior to motivate its repetition. In other words, find ways to self-motivate daily.

Why daily? Because the belief journey is a day-to-day process, 24/7, with no days off. At times, there are negative circumstances beyond our control. If we follow the steps of the belief system and persevere through them, then we deserve to self-reward and empower ourselves.

So, how do we establish daily positive reinforcements? The beauty of it is that you can create self-rewards. For example, if you achieved a physical workout you couldn't do a few months ago, simply congratulating yourself and journaling your success is a positive reinforcement. Or perhaps you passed a test you've been studying hard;

treating yourself to your favorite food stop is another example of positive reinforcement.

No matter how big or small the positive reinforcements are, it is important to make them a daily habit. Why? Think of the positive effects they can bring! When you practice positive reinforcements, they can lead to recurring positive habits, encourage a positive mindset, and trigger positive results. So, don't underestimate the power of positive reinforcements because they are essential in your overall belief journey.

Step IV: Final Step - Claim Your Belief

Whatever you believe in, whether it's your business, dreams, or even yourself, stand firm and claim your belief. Why claim it? Because it's yours. Nobody can take away your beliefs from you, and that's the beauty of it. So, how do you claim your beliefs?

Self-reflect: Take time to reflect on your values, strengths, and dreams so they remain at the forefront of your mind.

Celebrate achievements: Celebrate milestones and achievements. Recognizing positive results from your beliefs reinforces them.

Maintain commitment: Stay dedicated to your beliefs. Let no one sway you.

Inspire others: Share your beliefs and inspire others to do the same. Pay it forward.

When establishing a belief system or understanding what it truly means to have unwavering belief, I always think of the story **"The Little Engine That Could."** This timeless story holds a great message.

The Little Engine That Could is a story about the true meaning of belief. It begins with a long train needing to be pulled over a tall mountain after its locomotive stops working. The larger locomotives are asked to help, but they all make excuses and refuse.

However, the little engine doesn't give up. Despite what the others say, she firmly believes she can pull the train. She disregards the circumstances and focuses on the possibility. She establishes her purpose, eliminates negative mechanisms, establishes positive reinforcements, and claims her belief. With her unwavering mindset, she repeats, **"I think I can, I think I can."** And she does. She reaches the top of the mountain and, on the way down, celebrates her success by saying, **"I thought I could, I thought I could."**

We can all learn from **"The Little Engine That Could."** The most important lesson is that she held onto her belief steadfastly. Regardless of how impossible it seemed, she persevered and achieved what others deemed unattainable.

So after reading all this, you may be wondering, **"Ebony, what is the point of doing all this just to establish a belief system?"** Let me break it down for you real quick.

A **strong belief system** is the difference between moving with power or drifting aimlessly through life. It all starts with **PWR – Purpose, Why, and Reason**. Your **Purpose** gives you direction—it's the reason you wake up every day with intention. Your **Why** fuels you—it's that deep, personal fire that keeps you pushing forward even when things get tough. And your **Reason** is what keeps you solid—it's the logic, experience, and proof that backs up your belief. When all three align, you're **unshakable**. Without them? You're second-guessing, hesitating, and reacting instead of leading.

But let's be real—you can't fully step into your **PWR** if you're still carrying around **negative mechanisms**. That means breaking free from **self-doubt, fear, and toxic influences** that keep you stuck in cycles of uncertainty. It means silencing that little voice telling you you're not good enough and cutting off anything or anyone that's draining your energy. **You can't build a powerful mindset on a weak foundation.** When you remove the negativity, you make room for clarity, confidence, and real success.

Now, belief alone ain't enough—you have to **reinforce it daily**. This is where **daily positive reinforcements** come in. It's about consistently feeding your mind with **affirmations, intentional habits, and surrounding yourself with winners**. You don't just wake up successful—you build it, brick by brick, every single day. **Success is a habit, not a one-time event.** Stay locked in, stay focused, and keep reinforcing what you KNOW to be true about yourself.

And finally, it's time to **claim your belief**. Walk in it, own it, and stand firm in your truth. When you truly believe in yourself and your vision, doubt fades, and confidence takes over. **You don't need permission to be great—just the belief that you already are.** When you carry yourself with conviction, you become the blueprint—the example of what's possible when you operate in full alignment with your **PWR.**

So what's the point of doing all this? **Because this is how you stop hoping for success and start creating it.** This is how you develop **unshakable confidence, unstoppable momentum, and limitless elevation.** It's time to step into your power and own it.

So as we conclude Part I, I hope you understand the true meaning of belief. Belief isn't just a word we use to make ourselves feel better. To honestly believe, we must be ready to take action to reclaim our lives, dreams, and purpose.

So, before we move on to Part II, ask yourself: Are you ready to honestly believe? To believe like you never have before? If your answer is yes, I permit you to proceed to the next part of the formula: **G.R.I.N.D.**

The Belief System

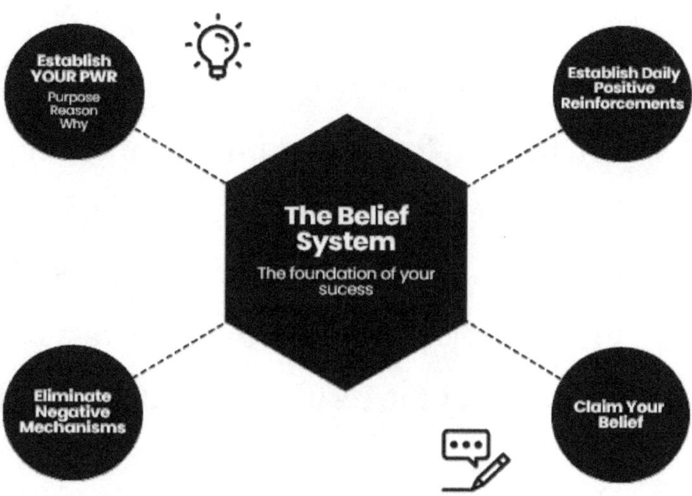

Exercise I: Establish Your Belief System

Before we proceed to Part II, there's an exercise I want you to complete. Yes, I understand I'm putting you to work, but then again, genuinely believing in yourself takes effort, so why delay when you can start now? As you engage in this brief exercise, feel free to do it with a partner. You might be surprised at the results you come up with!

Question 1: What is one thing you believe in? Is it a business idea? A dream? Write it down.

Question 2: Establish your PWR. Remember, a PWR consists of Purpose, Why, and Reason. Write down your PWR. Frame it. Save it. Repeat it to yourself each day.

Question 3: What bad habits do you need to eliminate? Secondly, how will you replace those bad habits to establish a positive mechanism?

Question 4: Establish daily positive reinforcements. Write them down and strive to practice them daily.

Part II: G.R.I.N.D

Grind. I often hear people say that every day is a grind. If you work harder now, you can play harder later. I will be honest. Whenever I think of the word "grind," it reminds me of that Rick Ross song. **"Every day, I'm hustling, every day I'm hustling, every day I'm hustling.** I must admit, I love this song. It got me pumped. It motivated me to get up, work hard, and pursue what I want out of life. So, every day, I started grinding, working hard, and going to the max. But after a while, I started to realize something. Every day, I was "hustling," "grinding," etc., but I still wasn't getting anywhere or achieving the desired results. I started to wonder, what was the whole point of me working this hard if it kept me at ground zero? Then suddenly, a lightbulb went off in my head.

Grinding is not just some type of formality; it is a mentality. Once you establish your belief system, it gives your "grind" a "focus. Grinding without a plan leaves your future uncertain. However, grinding with a "focus" gives your life the direction it needs in fulfilling your ultimate purpose.

Let's be honest. We all have people in our lives that we see grind all their lives. They work hard, but most of them haven't progressed or haven't pushed their purpose forward. Or maybe you have found yourself, grinding every day, working hard but seeing no movement towards your goals and the things you want to achieve. But why is this? It's simple. We put too much emphasis on **"the grind"** and not much emphasis on the **"outcome"**.

See, when you grind with a focus it leads to elevation. With the highest level of elevation, it converts into legacy, and with legacy, it creates an impact. The point that I am trying to make here is that you need to get to a point in your life where you grind because you **"want to"** not because you **"have to"**. Life is not meant for us to grind to the point where we cannot enjoy the fruits of labor or the impact that we can make on the world. The true purpose of grinding is to become a gateway to the fulfillment of our purpose.

Let's delve into this concept a bit deeper. When you hear the word "grind," what comes to mind? For most of us, it's not a pleasant image. The term "grinding" often brings up thoughts of struggling, of doing just enough to get by. But if we look at the true definition of grind, it means to oppress, torment, or crush. When you approach grinding with the wrong mindset, you're essentially tormenting yourself, crushing your dreams, and becoming your oppressor, blocking the path to your true purpose.

This pervasive, misguided mindset about grinding that we've all internalized is a subtle but powerful detriment. It distracts us from what it truly means to grind effectively and successfully, leading us to equate hard work with mere survival rather than purposeful progress.

Let me show you an example of how grinding ineffectively can produce adverse results.

Jackson Reynolds was the definition of hustle culture. A digital marketing consultant with big goals, he wore his 16-hour workdays like a badge of honor. From chasing down every lead to manually handling client projects, admin work, and late-night emails, he believed grinding non-stop was the only way to success. But despite his relentless efforts, he was stuck in the same revenue bracket—**making \$8K to \$10K per month,** constantly overwhelmed, and dangerously close to burnout.

The problem wasn't his ambition. It was the way he worked. Jackson was grinding in the wrong manner, believing that working harder meant making more money. Instead, he was exhausting himself on low-value tasks, operating without a system, and saying **"yes"** to every client instead of strategically positioning himself for growth. His business felt like a hamster wheel—running non-stop but going nowhere.

And then the real consequences started to hit. His mental and physical health took a dive—he barely slept, he was always stressed, and his creativity was shot. Clients sensed his frustration, and retention rates dropped because he couldn't provide the level of service he once promised. Worse, he started resenting his own business—the very thing he built with passion.

That's when he decided to make a shift. First, he automated and delegated anything that wasn't directly making him money. Scheduling, invoicing, and client management? He put systems in place. Emails and admin work? He hired a part-time project manager. With **40%** of his time freed up, he finally had room to focus on high-level strategy. Then, instead of taking on any and every client, he positioned himself as the go-to expert for high-ticket coaching businesses. That allowed him to double his rates while working with fewer clients. Finally, he stopped wasting time manually chasing leads. Instead, he built an automated LinkedIn and email outreach system that brought clients to him without his constant involvement.

The results? **Game-changing.** Within three months, Jackson's revenue jumped **from \$10K to \$25K per month**, and he was working half the hours. He wasn't just making more—he was working less, serving better clients, and finally scaling in a way that didn't leave him drained. His stress levels dropped, his business felt in control, and for the first time, he wasn't just grinding—he was growing.

But Jackson's experience isn't unique. Research backs up this shift in mindset. **A study by the American Psychological Association** found that multitasking due to overwork **reduces productivity by 40% and increases stress levels.** That means that the very hustle people believe is pushing them forward is actually pulling them back. Constantly jumping between tasks, answering emails while trying to complete deep work, and attempting to handle everything at once is a surefire way to slow down progress instead of accelerating it.

This is why success isn't about doing more—it's about doing what actually moves the needle. The key isn't grinding endlessly; it's making strategic moves that create sustainable, scalable results.

So, the real question we must ask ourselves is, "What is the correct way to grind?" Let's break down what "grind" truly means and explore how we approach it effectively and efficiently. Doing so can transform our efforts from a mere struggle to survive into a meaningful journey toward our goals.

As I thought about the word, **G.R.I.N.D,** I decided to break it down to understand its meaning.

G.R.I.N.D WITH PURPOSE

G. Get A Focus

The first step to effective grinding? Get a focus. Let me rewind to my college days—a full-time student with not one, but two work-study gigs: recycling tech by day, and research assistant by night. Oh, and did I mention my side hustle of trying to sell stuff online? All this while chasing my dream of becoming the next big entertainer. It was a recipe for burnout deluxe.

I distinctly remember the day exhaustion caught up with me so hard that I nearly passed out at my recycling station. My supervisor, bless her heart, saw me teetering on the brink of collapse and pulled me aside for a serious chat. **"Hey, superstar,"** she said, **"I admire your hustle, but you're spreading yourself thinner than dollar store toilet paper. You've got to focus on what matters—your dream of being an entertainer."**

Did I take her sage advice right then and there? Nope. I was too caught up in my **"grind mentality"** to slow down. Fast forward fourteen years, and let's just say I've had plenty of time to appreciate the wisdom in her words.

You see, grinding isn't the issue—it's crucial to work hard and pursue your goals with determination. But here's the catch: without a clear primary focus, all that effort can become scattered, leading to confusion, frustration, and ultimately, burnout.

Let's paint a picture. Ever met someone who seems to do it all? They hustle relentlessly—selling products, juggling multiple jobs, pursuing creative passions like recording music or photography, and even tutoring on the side. On the surface, it looks impressive. Yet, despite their hustle, they often find themselves overwhelmed and unsupported. They complain about lacking support, but the truth is, people around them struggle to provide it because they're unsure where to begin—the person's doing so much.

In their mind, they're hustling toward success, trying to make ends meet and inch closer to their dreams. But in reality, they're spreading themselves too thin. They're stuck in a cycle of distractions—tasks that don't align with their core ambitions. This lack of clarity leaves them feeling like they're moving forward when, in fact, they're just treading water.

What's missing? A clear, focused vision. By honing in on their primary goal and streamlining their efforts, they could channel their energy more effectively. It's about identifying what truly matters, shedding distractions, and paving a direct path toward their ultimate aspirations. That's the key to avoiding burnout and achieving sustainable success.

Here's the point: there's nothing wrong with holding a job or pursuing a side hustle or two, as long as they align with your primary focus or goal. For example, if your dream is to become a successful musician, it's fine to work a day job to support your passion. Use that time wisely—maybe hand out business cards or promote your music at work. You might also consider a side hustle, like selling branded merchandise or offering music lessons. This way, every effort supports your main goal, keeping you focused and aligned on your path to success.

Ultimately, the goal is to work smarter, not harder. Avoid overcomplicating your life by taking on too much and leaving no room to enjoy what's already there. With a focused grind, burnout becomes unnecessary.

R. Resist Old Habits

After you refocus yourself, do you know what the next biggest hurdle is? Relapsing into old habits. It's like trying to leave a party only to be pulled back in by the promise of cake. We all know how it goes: you start a diet to get healthier, and for the first few days, you're a health guru—eating right, counting calories, and even considering yoga. But then, the universe conspires against you. Food commercials, TikTok videos of people making gooey desserts, and the irresistible smell of fast food as you pass by on your way to work. Each day it gets harder to resist until you finally give in and feel like you've betrayed yourself.

Don't feel bad; we've all been there. Every time you get yourself back on track, something tries to lure you back to your old ways, like a siren call of snacks. So now, you might be wondering: how do you resist bad habits?

Here are some strategies, with a sprinkle of humor to keep things light:

1. **Identify Triggers:** Know what sets you off. Is it the sight of a cookie or the sound of a chip bag opening?

Recognize these triggers and prepare to face them like a ninja avoiding a pie to the face.

2. **Set Clear Goals:** Define what you want to achieve by breaking the bad habit. Think of it as your quest, like Frodo's journey to Mordor, but with fewer orcs and more kale.

3. **Develop a Plan:** Create a step-by-step plan to replace the bad habit with a healthier one. When tempted, do something else—maybe dance like nobody's watching. Actually, no, dance like everyone is watching. That should distract you.

4. **Stay Accountable:** Share your goals with a friend, family member, or support group. Make them your accountability buddy. You can even wear matching superhero capes for added motivation.

5. **Practice Self-Compassion:** Be kind to yourself if you slip up. Remember, even superheroes have bad days. Just pick yourself up, dust off the cookie crumbs, and keep going.

6. **Avoid Temptations:** Remove or minimize exposure to triggers. If you're trying to quit smoking, avoid places where you used to smoke. If chocolate is your

kryptonite, don't keep it in the house. Easy as pie... well, not pie. Pie is not allowed.

7. **Visualize Success:** Regularly visualize yourself successfully resisting the bad habit and enjoying the benefits of your new, healthier behavior. Picture yourself like a majestic swan, gliding past the chocolate fountain untempted.

8. **Track Progress:** Keep a journal or use an app to track your progress. Watching your journey from 'tempted by everything' to 'Zen master' is incredibly satisfying.

I. Indulge In Meditation

Grinding with focus is no walk in the park. It takes serious willpower to stay on track and chase those goals. But sometimes, people get so laser-focused that they forget to live a little. Hey, breathe. It's okay to take breaks along the way and enjoy life's little moments. Remember that thing called burnout? Yeah, you don't want to meet it, especially when you're cruising in the right direction. This is why I'm all about **INDULGING IN MEDITATION.**

Seriously, make meditation a regular part of your life, like second nature. Why? It teaches you to relax, recharge, and boost your energy. It helps you center your thoughts and avoid making decisions out of sheer panic or desperation. It realigns your emotions with logic so you can keep your focus on your goals. So, meditation is crucial for grinding effectively. Now, let me tell you how to meditate correctly so it contributes to your grind.

Find Your Quiet Space

- Pick a quiet spot where you won't be interrupted—bedroom, park, or even the bathroom if you have to.

Get Comfortable:

- Sit or lie down in a way that feels good. Think "relaxed but not ready for a nap."

Set a Timer:

- Start with 5-10 minutes. Enough time to chill, not enough to stress.

Close Your Eyes and Breathe:

- Close your eyes and take a few deep breaths. Inhale the good vibes, exhale the stress.

Focus on Your Breath:

- Notice the air going in and out. Pretend you're watching waves at the beach but in your lungs.

Thoughts Will Happen:

- Your brain will wander. It's okay. When it does, gently nudge it back to your breath like herding cats.

Use a Mantra (Optional):

- If it helps, repeat a word like "chill" or "om." Or even "pizza" if that keeps you happy.

Be Present:

- Notice what's happening now—sounds, sensations, your breath. No time-traveling to yesterday's worries or tomorrow's to-do list.

Wrap It Up:

- When the timer goes off, take a few deep breaths. Open your eyes slowly and return to reality, hopefully with more peace.

Make It a Habit:

- Try to do it around the same time each day. Think of it like brushing your teeth but for your brain.

N. Nurture Reality

You know the number one thing that happens when people are on the "grind"? They put unnecessary pressure on themselves. They chase after high expectations and set themselves up for failure. But here's the real question: who are you trying to impress? Family? Friends? Colleagues? Let me hit you with a hard truth—stop trying to impress others. Guess what? No one can live your life for you, and they sure can't die for you either.

Many people fall into a depressive state because they don't nurture their reality to prepare for the future. Listen, it's okay if you're not where you want to be. Day by day, step by step, you will get there. Accepting your reality helps you see how far you've come and how far you need to go. If you don't live in reality, your grind will become pointless, and you'll find yourself going in circles, never reaching your potential.

I get it. Most of us don't want to face our reality because we don't like it. We don't like our current situation, so we pretend it's not happening. But guess what? You have the power to change your reality, but first, you must accept it. So, let me tell you how to truly nurture your reality:

Set Realistic Goals:

- Aim for progress, not perfection. Remember, Rome wasn't built in a day, and neither is your dream life. Start small—maybe today's goal is just to get out of bed and put on pants. Baby steps.

Stay Positive:

- Surround yourself with positive people and limit exposure to negativity. It's like gardening—weed out the negativity and let the positivity bloom. And remember, every rose has its thorn, so a little prickly situation now and then is normal.

Stay Connected:

- Maintain strong relationships with friends and family. Social connections are like Wi-Fi for the soul—a better signal means a better life. Plus, who else is going to laugh at your terrible jokes?

Manage Stress:

- Find healthy ways to manage stress, like exercise, hobbies, or simply laughing at funny cat videos. Stress is a sneaky little gremlin; don't let it take over your life. If all else fails, just scream into a pillow—works wonders.

Express Gratitude:

- Regularly take time to appreciate what you have. Start a gratitude journal or just take a moment each day to reflect. Gratitude is like seasoning—life is bland without it. And hey, being thankful for your morning coffee is a solid start.

Embrace Change:

- Be flexible and open to change. Life's a rollercoaster; sometimes you just have to throw your hands up and enjoy the ride. And if you throw up, well, at least it's a story for later.

Set Boundaries:

- Learn to say no and protect your time and energy. Boundaries are like personal space bubbles—necessary for maintaining sanity. Think of it as building a fortress around your mental castle.

D. Drown Out Doubt

When you're on the **G.R.I.N.D**, the most crucial task is to silence doubt. Doubt is the number one obstacle we all face, and it often arises from fear. Let's be honest—life can be intimidating. The future is uncertain, and the road ahead is filled with unknowns, making us question what lies ahead. But remember, life is just a story, and you are the author. Whenever doubt creeps in, remind yourself that you are in control of your destiny. Don't let doubt take over, because it limits your potential and hides the true power within you.

Think about your favorite superhero—they face doubt all the time, but they push through it to achieve their goals. One of my favorite heroes is Goku from Dragon Ball. No matter what enemy or challenge he faces, he never lets fear or doubt stop him from saving and protecting the Earth. One of my favorite episodes of Dragon Ball Z is when Gohan battles Cell, a super android created to destroy Earth. Gohan was exhausted, severely injured, and barely holding onto his special attack against Cell. However, his father, Goku, was speaking to Gohan telepathically from "the other world," helping him overcome his doubt and fear to unleash his true power and defeat Cell. In the end, Gohan let go of his doubt, unlocked his true potential, and saved the Earth.

See yourself as your superhero. Just like Gohan, you have untapped potential and power within you, but doubt has held you back. Don't let doubt be the reason you don't reach your highest potential, and don't let it consume you. Want to know how to drown out doubt? Well, I'm about to show you how.

Embrace Challenges Like a New Adventure

Think of challenges as thrilling new adventures rather than dreaded obstacles. They're like the unexpected plot twists in your favorite adventure novel—exciting and full of potential. Instead of seeing them as roadblocks, view them as opportunities to test your skills and grow. Embrace the challenge with the same enthusiasm you'd have for an unexpected trip. When you face a tough situation, imagine you're gearing up for a wild ride and remember, every adventure has its ups and downs!

Celebrate Effort, Even If It's Not Perfect

Imagine you're working on a DIY project and it ends up looking a bit lopsided. Instead of stressing over the imperfections, give yourself credit for diving in and giving it a go. Celebrating your effort, rather than just the result, helps you appreciate the journey. Think of it like giving yourself a "Participant" ribbon—it's all about trying and learning. So, high-five yourself for the effort and keep going, because every attempt is a step closer to mastering the craft.

Take Action, Even If You're Not Sure

Ever found yourself stuck in a cycle of overthinking, like trying to decide which restaurant to choose and ending up eating the same old thing? Sometimes, you just need to take a leap and make a choice, even if you're not entirely sure. Taking action, even when you're a bit uncertain, helps you move forward and gain clarity. It's like taking a bite of a new dish—you might not know if you'll love it, but you won't find out until you try it. So go ahead and make the move; you'll figure things out as you go and leave the self-doubt in the dust.

As a matter of fact, let me give you a powerful example of someone who truly understood the real meaning of **G.R.I.N.D.**

When I hear the word **G.R.I.N.D**, the first person who comes to mind is my late maternal grandfather, Clement Luckett, Sr. My grandfather was a true Renaissance man and the hardest worker I've ever known. He was an entrepreneur in every sense of the word—driving trucks as an owner-operator, running a lawn care business, managing real estate, and more. It's from him that I believe I inherited my entrepreneurial spirit.

My grandfather's approach to grinding was rooted in his unwavering commitment to providing and protecting his family. His focus never wavered, even through health challenges. Despite heart issues, he adapted his lifestyle, improved his eating habits, and managed stress to keep doing what he loved: supporting his family. His unique way of meditating was simply sitting in the garage, relaxing, reflecting, and having deep conversations. Those garage sessions were filled with valuable life lessons, and I cherish our shared moments.

One thing I admired about my grandfather was his realism. He didn't chase unattainable dreams; instead, he focused on achievable goals and never pressured himself into doing what he couldn't handle. That's how he kept self-doubt at bay. He used to say that life wasn't meant to be easy but was full of lessons to teach us how to overcome adversity. My grandfather faced life head-on, appreciated the small things, and never strived for perfection but always gave his best effort.

Whenever I feel exhausted from my grind, I think of my grandfather. He never gave up, working hard until he could no longer do so. His passing in 2018 left a hole in my heart, but his impact remains with me. Thanks to the example he set, I've learned what it truly means to grind successfully.

With the example of my grandfather I just shared, it shows one thing: **grinding with a purpose yields results.** It's not just about working hard—it's about working **smart and strategic.** A study by McKinsey & Company backs this up, proving that individuals who lock in on deep work and **high-impact tasks** are **500% more productive** than those who stay stuck in the cycle of busywork and multitasking. That's the difference between **grinding aimlessly** and **grinding with intention**—one burns you out, the other builds you up.

As we wrap up this section, let's acknowledge that grinding isn't a walk in the park—neither is achieving success. But when you approach your grind with genuine focus, things start to fall into place, and the path ahead becomes clearer. Each day is a fresh chance to inch closer to your ultimate goal. Set realistic expectations, stay focused, and embrace your imperfections. Our mistakes are just little lessons that reveal more about our strengths and weaknesses. The aim isn't perfection but to let our imperfections shape us, helping us keep grinding and moving toward success.

With a better understanding of what grinding truly entails, it's time for a quick exercise before we dive into the final part of the B.G.C formula—**CONSISTENCY**.

Exercise II: Evaluate Your G.R.I.N.D

Before we dive into Part III, take a moment to evaluate your grind. I know, more work, but remember, hard work pays off in the long run! As you answer these questions, be brutally honest with yourself. This self-assessment will help you understand just how effective your grind is.

Question 1: What specific goals or tasks did you identify today as your primary focus, and what strategies did you use to stay concentrated on them?

Question 2: Which old habits or distractions did you actively work to avoid today, and how did you handle moments when they tempted you?

Question 3: How did you incorporate meditation or mindfulness practices into your day, and what impact did it have on your overall productivity and mindset?

Question 4: How did you engage with and adapt to the reality of your current situation or environment, and what steps did you take to align your actions with your present circumstances?

Question 5: What strategies or affirmations did you use today to overcome self-doubt or uncertainty, and how did they affect your confidence and decision-making?

Question 6: How did you measure your progress or success today with your focus goals, and what adjustments did you make based on your experiences?

Part III: CONSISTENCY

It's often said that if you want to get good at something, you need to be consistent. **Consistency**—it's a word we hear all the time, but what does it mean? Generally, consistency means sticking to the same principles, actions, or habits over time. For instance, every morning, my husband and I make it a routine to pray together, setting a positive tone for our day. Because we do this consistently, it's now second nature to us.

But just because you're consistent doesn't necessarily mean it's beneficial. Take, for example, consistently practicing poor eating habits; it can lead to unwanted health issues. This highlights an important point: there's good consistency and bad consistency. Let's break down the difference between the two.

What is Bad Consistency?

Let's talk about **Bad Consistency**—and trust me, I know this one all too well. Consistency can be a powerful tool, but it's not always working in your favor. Sometimes, it keeps you in cycles that feel comfortable but lead nowhere.

Let me give you an example: I was ***consistently*** practicing overachieving. Restless nights, no mental break, constant worrying—it became my routine. I was always pushing, always going, thinking it was the path to success. But where did it lead me? Burnout, depression, and feeling like a failure. I was pouring everything into a cycle that didn't elevate me—it exhausted me. I realized I was caught in **bad consistency**—a cycle of behaviors that felt productive but didn't take me anywhere new. Just circles.

Bad consistency keeps you in patterns that are familiar but limit you in the long run. You keep doing them because they're comfortable, but they lead to setbacks, not progress. Let's look at a few examples of how this can show up:

1. **Self-Sabotaging Habits**
   You know those **"I'll do it tomorrow"** days? Putting things off, avoiding the hard stuff, or talking yourself down. These habits seem small but build up over time, keeping you from stepping into your power. Consistently putting things off builds a habit of

self-limitation, like tying weights to your potential and wondering why you're not flying.

2. **Unhealthy Lifestyle Choices**

   It's easy to fall into comfortable choices with your health—like skipping the workout, going for a quick snack, or ignoring sleep. These choices seem harmless in the moment, but over time they add up, affecting your energy, mood, and health. This kind of consistency puts limits on your life and holds back the energy you need to thrive.

3. **Toxic Relationship Patterns**

   Then there are the relationships. Consistently letting toxic behavior slide or sacrificing yourself to keep the peace—that's bad consistency too. It chips away at your confidence and creates patterns where you lose yourself in others instead of building relationships that lift you higher.

4. **Stagnation in Personal Growth**

   Sometimes, being **"consistent"** is just staying comfortable and avoiding challenges. When you're consistently avoiding growth, you're avoiding greatness. This kind of consistency is a slow killer of progress and resilience, keeping you in a comfort zone that's anything but comfortable in the long run.

5. **Reinforcing Negative Mindsets**
   And let's not forget the power of mindset. If you're consistently feeding yourself negative thoughts—**"I'm not good enough," "I can't do it,"**—you're building a reality that reflects those thoughts. This kind of bad consistency limits your potential and keeps you stuck.

Bad Consistency Formula:

So, let's put this all into a formula. Here's what bad consistency looks like:

(Short-Term Comfort + Negative Actions) x Repetition = Long-Term Setbacks

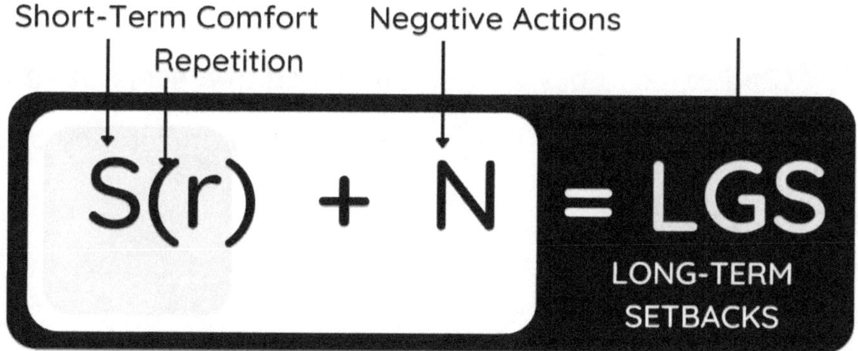

Breaking it down:

- **Short-Term Comfort** – This is the hook. Bad consistency feels good or easy at the moment, like procrastinating, avoiding tough conversations, or sticking to your usual routine, even if it's not working.

- **Negative Actions** – These are actions that don't line up with your goals. They might feel small, but they're the seeds of setbacks. Whether it's hours spent scrolling social media, eating mindlessly, or doubting yourself, these choices don't support your growth.

- **Repetition** – Consistency's real power is in repetition, but here it's the wrong kind of repetition. These small, comfortable choices build on each other, creating a routine that doesn't elevate you.

- **Long-Term Setbacks** – This is where it all leads. Those little comfortable choices, day by day, snowball into missed opportunities, health issues, and wasted potential. It's like running in circles but never moving forward.

Bad consistency keeps you locked in place, but you deserve more. Let me show you what bad consistency can do to your dreams.

Marcus had a dream—he wanted to build a thriving consulting business. He had the skills, the knowledge, and even the network to make it happen. But instead of committing to the right habits, he fell into the comfort of bad consistency.

At first, it started small. He would procrastinate on lead generation because he convinced himself that his existing network was **"enough."** He prioritized short-term comfort—binge-watching Netflix, scrolling through social media—over the disciplined actions that would drive growth. The negative actions crept in: missing follow-ups, ignoring marketing efforts, failing to track his finances. But he told himself, **"I'll get serious next month."**

And then came repetition. One month turned into three. Three turned into a year. Every day, Marcus reinforced the same self-sabotaging patterns. The more he delayed action, the harder it became to break free. His pipeline dried up. Revenue plummeted. The reputation he once had began to fade because people saw the inconsistency in his business. Instead of owning his mistakes and pivoting, he doubled down on excuses.

By the time Marcus realized what had happened, it was too late. The long-term setback had already taken root. His once-promising consulting firm was now drowning in debt, with no clients in sight. The worst part? The downfall wasn't because of external forces—it was because of the choices he had unknowingly reinforced day after day.

Bad consistency is just as powerful as good consistency—but in the opposite direction. And for Marcus, the price of repetition was the death of his business.

Success doesn't happen overnight, but neither does failure. Every small decision compounds over time. If you keep reinforcing the wrong habits, don't be surprised when they become the reason you lose everything. A study by Duke University found that **about 45% of our daily behaviors are driven by habits, not conscious decisions.** If you're not intentional about your actions, your default habits—good or bad—will determine your success or failure.

This is your invitation to shift, to break out of bad consistency, and to build patterns that empower you. Make the change to habits that work FOR you, not against you.

What is Good Consistency?

We've talked about **Bad Consistency**, so let's talk about **Good Consistency**—the kind that elevates, drives real progress, and transforms dreams into reality. Good consistency is where we create momentum, aligning with purpose and passion to move forward. It's not just about doing the same things over and over—it's about doing the *right* things, in a way that builds and sustains success.

Here's a perfect example: I think back to my childhood, watching my mother go back to school. Let me set the scene—it was five of us, all involved in different activities, and my youngest sibling was just a toddler. Yet my mother did it. To this day, I'm amazed at how she managed. She practiced **good consistency**: keeping a tight schedule, prioritizing her family, and still finding time for her classes and homework. And because of that consistency, she didn't just complete school; she went on to earn multiple degrees. That's the power of good consistency—it's disciplined, aligned, and keeps you moving forward.

Good consistency is about creating patterns that support your growth and align with your goals. It's doing the work, day in and day out, in a way that's sustainable and purpose-driven. Let's look at what it takes to build good consistency:

1. **Purposeful Actions**

   Good consistency starts with intentional actions. When you're focused on goals that matter, every action serves a purpose. You're not just busy—you're building. Like my mother, who didn't waste a single moment; everything she did aligned with her priorities, her family, and her education.

2. **Discipline Over Motivation**

   Let's be real—motivation fades, but discipline sticks around. Good consistency doesn't rely on feeling **"inspired"** every day. Instead, it's about showing up, rain or shine, even when you don't feel like it. Consistency in discipline creates progress that lasts, even when the initial spark of excitement wears off.

3. **Focused Prioritization**

   With good consistency, you know where to focus. It's about saying **"yes"** to what matters most and **"no"** to distractions. My mother knew her priorities: family and education. She protected her time and energy, only investing in what aligned with her goals. When you're consistent with what matters, you build momentum toward success.

4. **Adaptability and Flexibility**

   Good consistency isn't rigid. Life happens, and plans change, but good consistency adapts without falling off track. If you miss a day, you don't throw in the towel—you adjust and keep going. It's consistency that's flexible enough to adjust while staying aligned with the big picture.

5. **Small Wins, Big Results**

   Good consistency understands the power of small, repeated actions. Those small steps build on each other, compounding into powerful results over time. It's not about massive leaps—it's about steady steps that, together, create the transformation you're after.

Good Consistency Formula:

GOOD CONSISTENCY FORMULA

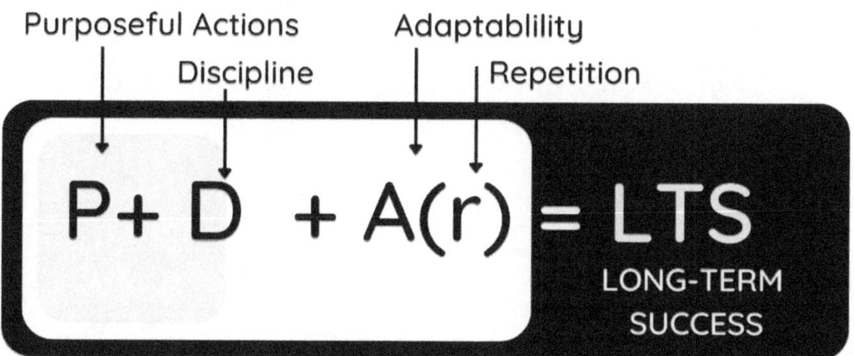

Here's the formula for good consistency, the kind that builds success:

(Purposeful Actions + Discipline + Adaptability) x Repetition = Long-Term Success

Let's break it down:

- **Purposeful Actions** – Every action is intentional and aligns with your goals. You're not just doing things for the sake of it—you're building something meaningful.
- **Discipline** – This is the backbone of good consistency. You keep showing up, even when motivation fades. Discipline is what makes consistency sustainable.
- **Adaptability** – Good consistency stays flexible. When things get tough, you adapt and keep going. You're not derailed by setbacks; you find ways to keep moving forward.
- **Repetition** – It's the repetition of aligned, disciplined actions that creates the magic. Day by day, these actions stack up, leading to real growth and transformation.

- **Long-Term Success** – The result? Success that lasts. With good consistency, you're building a foundation that supports your goals for the long haul.

Good consistency is the path to lasting change. It's about elevating your habits and aligning your actions with your vision. When you practice good consistency, you're investing in yourself and your future, one powerful step at a time. Let's build that momentum—because every step forward brings you closer to who you're meant to be.

The Million Dollar Question

Alright, here's the million-dollar question: **"Ebony, how do you stay consistent in *being consistent*?"** Now, when you first read that, it might sound a bit silly—but think about it. It's not silly at all. Staying consistent is hard! Life throws challenges our way, problems pop up out of nowhere, and let's be real—sometimes we just get lazy. I've been guilty of that too, so no judgment here.

So, the real question is: how do we stay consistent at *being* consistent?

Alright, let's get real: staying consistent in *being* consistent? That's no easy feat! But trust me, it's possible with the right mindset, a little humor, and a whole lot of heart. So let's break down how to build that rock-solid foundation to keep you moving forward, even when life gets a little wild.

1. Know Your 'Why' Like It's Your Best Friend

Your **'why'** is your anchor. This isn't just some fluffy idea; this is what pulls you out of bed when you'd rather hit snooze for the fifth time. So, get clear on why consistency matters. Is it for that financial freedom you keep dreaming about? For the impact you want to make? Write it down, frame it, and make it loud and proud. When your 'why' is strong enough, excuses start sounding weak.

2. Break It Down Like a Boss

Look, you don't have to conquer Everest on day one. Consistency works best when you keep it bite-sized. Break those big goals down into smaller, snackable steps. Hit those mini-goals weekly or monthly so you can stack those wins. It's about building confidence one step at a time. Plus, there's nothing like celebrating a small win to remind you that you're on track.

3. Set Up a Routine and Guard It Like Gold

Consistency craves structure. Build a routine that works with your life—not one that feels like a punishment. Block out time for what matters and stick to it. Get into a rhythm that fits you, but keep it flexible. A good routine is like a playlist that lifts you up but can still switch tracks when life throws a curveball.

4. Get a Little Accountability Going

Accountability is magic for consistency. Find a friend, mentor, or even a nosy family member who'll check in and keep you honest. And don't underestimate the power of tools! Grab a habit-tracker, and set reminders—whatever keeps you in line. Because let's be real, sometimes just knowing someone's watching your progress keeps you moving.

5. Expect Life to Throw You a Few Curveballs

Life can be messy, and setbacks are a part of the game. But here's the trick: don't let a little chaos knock you off track. Plan for those "off" days. If you miss a day, don't let it turn into a week. If you hit a rough patch, don't throw in the towel—adjust and keep going. This way, you're not just consistent; you're resilient, too.

6. Build Discipline Like It's Your Superpower

Here's the truth: motivation is fickle. It's here today, gone tomorrow. Discipline, though? That's your ride-or-die. Start with small, daily commitments that build up your discipline muscle. Even on the days you don't feel like it, show up. That's how you build consistency that lasts—by relying on discipline, not just fleeting motivation.

7. Celebrate Every Win Like It's Your Birthday

Consistency isn't about perfection; it's about progress. So every little win? Celebrate it. Did you show up today? Celebrate. Did you hit a mini-goal? Celebrate. These small victories remind you that you're moving forward, and that's what consistency is all about. Make it fun, and you'll want to keep going.

8. Fuel Your Energy, Protect Your Mindset

You can't stay consistent if your tank is empty. Take care of your body with rest, good food, and movement. Keep your mind strong, too—surround yourself with people and influences that lift you up, not weigh you down. A strong, positive mindset is the foundation for consistency, so guard it like a fortress.

9. Check Yourself and Adjust as Needed

Being consistent doesn't mean sticking to something that isn't working. Review your goals regularly and make adjustments where needed. Consistency should feel like you're building, not draining. If something feels off, change it up. Remember, flexibility within consistency is powerful—it keeps you aligned and refreshed.

10. Commit to the Long Game

Consistency is the ultimate long game. It's like planting seeds and nurturing them over time. There will be days it feels slow like you're not getting anywhere, but trust the process. Consistency compounds—those small actions add up to big results. So stick with it, even when it feels like nothing's happening. Every step forward is building the future you want.

In the end, staying consistent in being consistent is all about setting yourself up for success and embracing the journey. Don't stress the slip-ups; they're part of the process. Keep your 'why' close, celebrate your progress, and show up—even when it's tough. Because consistency isn't about being perfect; it's about being committed. Keep showing up, and watch the magic unfold!

The Ultimate Legend of Good Consistency

Alright, let's talk about one of the ultimate legends of good consistency—**Walt Disney** himself. This man was a masterclass in *being consistent at being consistent*, and he didn't just talk about dreams; he built a whole world out of them!

Picture this: Walt started with nothing but a drawing of a little mouse, a vision, and a refusal to quit. But let's be real—Walt didn't have it easy. He faced bankruptcy, was told his ideas would never work, and even had his first major character *stolen* from him. Did he give up? Nope. He stayed consistent in his vision and actions, pushing forward when most people would have thrown in the towel and maybe taken up knitting.

1. Purposeful Actions with a Vision Bigger than His Critics

Walt knew his 'why' and kept it front and center. Every day, he worked with a purpose: to create a place that sparked imagination and happiness. He wasn't just drawing cartoons; he was building a world of storytelling and innovation that had never been seen before. When people told him he was crazy, he didn't stop—he doubled down. *Good consistency* was in every decision he made because he wasn't just working; he was working toward something magical.

2. Discipline Over Distractions

Walt had plenty of reasons to quit—failed projects, financial disasters, and people in suits telling him he'd never succeed. But his discipline was rock solid. Even on the hard days, he showed up. He took rejection and used it as fuel. I mean, this man was consistent in *proving people wrong*! The world said "no," but Walt kept saying "Watch me."

3. Focused Prioritization, No Time for Naysayers

Walt Disney was laser-focused. He wasn't out there trying to make everyone happy or prove himself to the doubters—he was too busy making history. He protected his time, prioritized his dream, and only invested in what aligned with his vision. *Good consistency* for Walt meant keeping his priorities straight, even when people laughed at the idea of a "theme park." Now look who's laughing.

4. Adaptability Like a Pro

Life threw Walt some *serious* curveballs. The man lost Oswald the Lucky Rabbit, and instead of calling it quits, he created a little character called Mickey Mouse. His business went bankrupt, so he adapted and came up with new projects. Walt's brand of consistency didn't mean sticking to a rigid plan—it meant sticking to the vision, no matter how many times he had to adjust along the way.

5. Celebrating Wins and Building Momentum

Even the small wins mattered to Walt. Every success fueled the next one, and he celebrated each step by pushing for more. He didn't wait for one big moment of glory; he built his dream, piece by piece, brick by brick. And every little achievement was another step toward creating Disney Studios, Disneyland, and the empire we know today.

The Good Consistency Formula—Walt Disney Style

Here's Walt's formula for good consistency in action:

(Purposeful Actions + Discipline + Adaptability) x Repetition = Magic and Legacy

Breaking it down:

- **Purposeful Actions** – Walt didn't just work; he worked *with purpose.* He was all-in, every day, making moves that aligned with his dream of building a world of imagination.
- **Discipline** – Even when things looked bleak, Walt showed up. He pushed through every "no," every failure, with the kind of discipline that never goes out of style.
- **Adaptability** – Disney was all about adjusting his plans without giving up the dream. He knew how to roll with the punches and create something new out of every setback.

- **Repetition** – Day after day, he repeated these actions, and that's where the magic happened. One consistent step at a time, he built a legacy that inspires millions today.

Walt Disney is proof that good consistency isn't about luck or perfection—it's about showing up, adapting, and never losing Matter of fact, a study by the American Psychological Association found that **people who set specific goals and stay consistent in working toward them are 42% more likely to succeed than those who don't even track their progress.** Success ain't magic—it's the result of showing up, putting in the work, and letting small wins stack up over time. You can't just "hope" your way to the top; you gotta be consistent and intentional if you want real results.

So here we are, at the end of this section. We've covered consistency from every angle—***bad consistency*** that holds us back, and ***good consistency*** that lifts us. This isn't just about a buzzword or some fancy concept; consistency is the foundation that determines whether you're building your dreams or just daydreaming.

So here's the big takeaway: **consistency is power**. But not just any power—*it's the power to create the life you want or the life you're willing to settle for*. When you're consistent with the right actions, that's where the magic is. It's not glamorous, and it's not always exciting. It's the daily grind, the small habits, and the discipline that makes greatness possible.

Bad consistency is that sneaky trap that keeps you in your comfort zone, doing the same old things that feel easy but lead nowhere. It's hitting snooze five times, it's pushing off your goals **"until tomorrow,"** it's that mindset that's just happy to stay on autopilot. Sure, it feels comfortable now, but in the long run, bad consistency is a thief. It steals your potential, your confidence, and your dreams. You're running in circles, thinking you're making moves but never really getting anywhere.

Good consistency, though? Now, *that's where the real transformation happens*. Good consistency is building those positive, purposeful habits. It's knowing your 'why' and using it to fuel every action, even on the hard days. It's the commitment to show up when you're tired, to stay focused when distractions hit, and to keep going when you feel like giving up. This is where champions are made—not in the big wins, but in the small, consistent steps that get you there.

Think of good consistency as planting seeds. You won't see results overnight, but with every intentional step, you're watering those seeds, nurturing them, and watching them grow into something powerful. Good consistency takes patience and vision, but let me tell you, it's worth every single step.

And here's the real secret: it's not just about being consistent; it's about being consistent in ***staying consistent***. That's the next level. You see, anyone can be motivated for a day, a week, maybe even a month. But the ones who reach their dreams are the ones who know how to keep going when the motivation fades. It's about building that rock-solid foundation so that even when life gets messy, you're still moving forward. Consistency is your safety net, your power source, and your ladder to every goal you're chasing.

If there's one thing I want you to take away, it's this: consistency isn't perfection; it's commitment. It's not about never slipping up; it's about refusing to quit. You will have setbacks, distractions, and days when it feels impossible—but those are the days when consistency counts the most. Those are the moments where you prove to yourself that your dreams are stronger than any excuse, any obstacle, or any setback.

Good consistency will lead you to growth, success, and fulfillment. Bad consistency? It'll leave you stuck. The choice is yours to make every day, with every action. So let's commit to that *good consistency*—to showing up, leveling up, and creating a life that feels like magic because you put in the work to build it.

Stay consistent, stay resilient, and keep moving forward. Remember, you're not just creating habits; you're creating the future you deserve. And if you ever feel like giving up, just remind yourself: ***the world didn't get Disney without a little bit of crazy, consistent vision***. Go all in, stay true to your path, and let's make your dreams happen—one consistent step at a time!

Exercise III: Reinforcing Consistency

We've just wrapped up the last section of the book! But before we dive into the conclusion, I have one more exercise for you to tackle. I know, I know—you're probably thinking, "Another exercise? Really?" But if you've truly been absorbing what you've read so far, you'll understand why this is essential. Let's put all that knowledge into action and make it stick!

Question 1: What is your 'why' behind your main goal, and how can keeping this in mind help you stay consistent?

Question 2: Reflect on your habits: List two examples of 'bad consistency' in your life. How do these habits hold you back from reaching your goals?

Question 3: Describe one area where you already practice 'good consistency.' How does this help you grow or make progress?

Question 4: What are three small, achievable goals you can commit to daily or weekly to build 'good consistency' toward your main goal?

Question 5: What are some potential setbacks or obstacles you might face while staying consistent? How will you adapt to keep going when these arise?

Question 6: How will you celebrate small wins to keep yourself motivated and build momentum? Give an example of a small milestone you can reward yourself for achieving.

The Finale

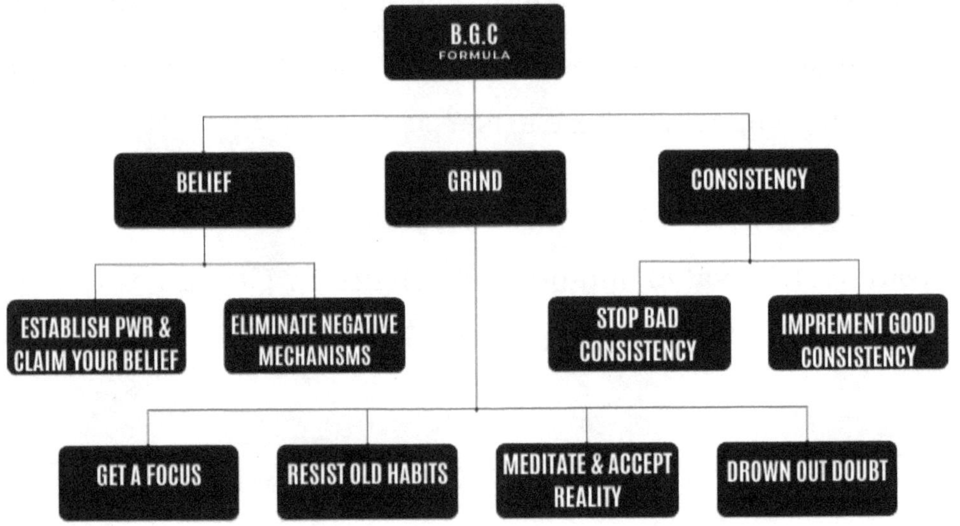

We've reached the end of the journey—**Belief, Grind, and Consistency.** You've made it through the exercises and dug into the mindset shifts, and now it's time to bring it all together. Let's get real about what this book is all about unlocking the power of *who you are*, what you believe, and the work you're willing to put in to make your dreams a reality. This isn't just some **"rah-rah"** self-help cheerleading—this is about creating a solid foundation for real, lasting change.

Belief: The Spark That Starts It All

Let's start with **belief**—the ultimate fuel for everything. Belief is where dreams are born, where goals start to breathe. But this isn't just any kind of belief; it's that deep, unshakeable belief in yourself. It's knowing that, no matter how big the vision, you're built to make it happen. Think of it as the foundation beneath everything else, that *silent strength* inside that tells you, "I got this." Without belief, we're just running in circles. With it? We're unstoppable.

Belief isn't about ignoring reality or pretending things are perfect. It's about trusting yourself through the ups and downs, and believing in your worth even when the world says otherwise. It's the courage to step up, to keep going when everyone else has tapped out, and to know that every setback is just a setup for something greater. When you own your belief, you own your future. Period.

Grind: The Work Behind the Dream

Now, belief is powerful, but let's not kid ourselves—**belief without the grind is just wishful thinking**. And we don't do wishful thinking around here; we do *the work*. The grind is where you take that belief and back it up with action. It's those early mornings, late nights, and the moments when you're pushing through, even when you'd rather be anywhere else.

But here's the beauty of the grind—it's not just about hustling until you're burnt out. It's about putting in smart, intentional work that moves you closer to your vision. Grinding isn't glamorous; it's real, it's raw, and sometimes, it's downright hard. But it's also incredibly rewarding because every step forward builds that momentum. Every small action, every bit of progress, is proof that you're getting closer to what you want. Grinding isn't punishment—it's empowerment. It's the journey you take to become the best version of yourself.

Consistency: The Key to Long-Term Success

And then we have **consistency**—the glue that holds it all together. Consistency is the daily commitment to show up, to keep moving, and to stay true to the path. It's easy to be motivated for a week, maybe even a month. But true success? That comes when you're consistent in the *long game.* It's about showing up even when motivation is nowhere to be found, even when you're tired, even when the goal feels a million miles away.

Consistency is that quiet power. It's the unshakeable force that turns good days and bad days into progress. And look, I get it—staying consistent is hard! Life throws you curveballs, people let you down, and sometimes, Netflix just looks *so much* better than your to-do list. But this is where champions are made. Champions are the ones who keep going, who keep grinding, who stay true to the mission day after day, step after step.

Pulling It All Together

So, here's the real deal: if you're willing to *believe in yourself,* to put in the *grind,* and to stay *consistent,* there is no limit to what you can achieve. You have everything you need to make your dreams a reality—it's been within you all along. This journey isn't about finding something outside yourself; it's about uncovering the strength, the courage, and the determination that's already there.

Now, I'm not saying the road will be easy because let's be honest—it won't be. There will be days when it feels like you're moving backward, moments when the goal seems out of reach, and times when you wonder why you even started. But those are the moments that will define you. Those are the moments when you'll prove to yourself just how strong you are. Keep believing, keep grinding, and keep showing up—because the life you want is on the other side of that consistency.

Final Words

As you close this book, remember: **You're the author of your story, and the pen is in your hand.**

Write a story that's worth telling. Write a story that reflects your courage, your resilience, and your vision. Don't settle for halfway. Don't let setbacks or doubts steal your dreams. You've got the tools, the power, and the drive—now it's up to you to make it happen.

So go out there, be bold, stay focused, and above all, be consistent in showing up as the best version of yourself. You're ready for this. And whenever you need a reminder, just come back to these pages, because you've already got everything you need to make it happen. Now let's go make magic, one consistent step at a time.

About The Author

Ebony "The Ebonizer" Baylock is an award-winning entertainer, speaker, and business powerhouse, known for her fierce energy, motivational spirit, and commitment to empowering others. As a sales and growth expert, Ebony has worked with numerous companies —helping them unlock their full potential through a focus on sustainable revenue growth and brand elevation. She's the founder of *Music Evolved Records & Ebonized Me*, a company that guides businesses through her unique BLSE Model **(Build, Launch, Scale, Elevate)**,

With a rich background that includes performing on stages with Yolanda Adams, Nick Carter, and Celine Dion as an alumna of Walt Whitman's ***The Soul Children of Chicago,*** Ebony's charisma and passion shine through everything she does. Known as "The Ebonizer," she brings a powerful blend of business acumen, creative flair, and motivational grit to the table, dedicated to helping others change their mindsets, grow their brands, and achieve their dreams. Ebony's work is deeply rooted in helping clients unlock their potential, harness their strengths, and create lasting success.

You can follow **The Ebonizer** and stay connected with her journey at:

- www.imtheebonizer.online
- www.ebonizeme.com